31 Declarations of Truth

Based on the Scriptures
Bisi Oladipupo

Springs of life publishing

Copyright © 2025 by Bisi Oladipupo

Springs of life publishing

ISBN: 978-1-915269-50-8 (ePub e-book)

ISBN: 978-1-915269-51-5 (paperback)

All Rights Reserved.

No part of this book may be used or reproduced by any means, graphic, electronic, or mechanical, including photocopying, recording, taping, or by any information storage retrieval system without the written permission of the publisher except in the case of brief quotations embodied in critical articles and reviews.

Printed in the United Kingdom

Unless otherwise indicated, scripture quotations are taken from the New King James Version.

Scripture taken from the New King James Version®. Copyright © 1982 by Thomas Nelson. Used by permission. All rights reserved.

Scripture quotations from The Authorized (King James) Version. Rights in the Authorized Version in the United Kingdom are vested in the Crown. Reproduced by permission of the Crown's patentee, Cambridge University Press.

Scripture quotations marked (AMP) are taken from the Amplified Bible, Copyright © 2015 by The Lockman Foundation. Used by permission.

31 DECLARATIONS OF TRUTH

Contents

Foreword	VIII
Introduction	X
1. I Have Eternal Life	1
2. I Am Endued With Power From on High	3
3. I Have Received His Fulness	5
4. Called Into the Fellowship of His Son	7
5. The Prince of Peace Lives in Me	9
6. The Father of Mercies Is My Father	11
7. I Am a King and Priest Unto God	13
8. The Lord Makes a Way	15
9. The Path of the Just Shines Brighter and Brighter	17

10.	I Reign in Life Through Christ Jesus	19
11.	I Have the Mind of Christ	21
12.	I Am One Spirit With the Lord	23
13.	Surely, Goodness and Mercy Shall Follow Me	25
14.	No Condemnation in Christ Jesus	27
15.	Christ Is Glorified in Me	29
16.	Joint Heirs With Christ	31
17.	Partaker of the Heavenly Calling	33
18.	Seated in Heavenly Places With Christ	35
19.	The Lord Is My Helper	37
20.	The Blessing of Abraham	39
21.	I Will Not Bring Forth for Sorrow	41
22.	As He Is, so Are We in This World	43
23.	I Am a Chosen Generation, a Royal Priesthood, a Holy Nation, a Peculiar People	45
24.	The Spirit of Truth Dwells in Me	47

25.	I Am the Righteousness of God in Christ Jesus	49
26.	The Grace of God Is at Work in Me	51
27.	The Generation of the Upright Is Blessed	53
28.	Jesus Loves Me as the Father Loves Jesus	55
29.	God Always Causes Me to Triumph in Christ	57
30.	I Am Crucified With Christ	59
31.	God Is Not Withholding His Will From Me	61
Acknowledgements		63
About the author		64
Salvation Prayer		65
Also by Bisi		67
Afterword		70

Foreword

What a blessing to read this short but practical guide, which reminds us of the power of the tongue and the wisdom in speaking words of life.

Words that will shape our lives and destinies for the good as believers in the Lord Jesus Christ

This comes as a handy daily devotional as we take each of the prayers, verbalise them, and see them change

It is also beneficial as a reference source for prayers that depict the truth of God's word

This book is highly recommended.

Pastor Sunday Oke, Senior Pastor, Sureway International Christian Ministries, Malta

Introduction

Why declarations of truth?

The Scriptures tell us something very important about the tongue:

"Death and life *are* in the power of the tongue, And those who love it will eat its fruit" (Proverbs 18:21).

This tells us that our tongues are very powerful. What we say can produce life and death. The scripture further tells us that those who love it will eat its fruit. In other words, we will eat the fruit of our tongues.

As wise people, we will choose to speak life and therefore eat the fruit of life. This is the whole purpose of declarations of truth.

Jesus Christ, our Lord and Saviour, during His earthly ministry, told us that the words that He speaks are spirit and life (John 6:63).

The scripture tells us a lot about speaking:

"(For assuredly, I say to you, whoever says to this mountain, 'Be removed and be cast into the sea,' and does not doubt in his heart, but believes that those things he says will be done, he will have whatever he says" (Mark 11:23).

'And since we have the same spirit of faith, according to what is written, "I believed and therefore I spoke," we also believe and therefore speak' (2 Corinthians 4:13).

If you notice from these two scriptures, the action that precedes speaking is believing. When we believe what we want to say, it is then that we speak.

Could this be where many have got this wrong? We must believe what we are saying before we say it, for it to produce results.

We also need to remember that fruit takes time. It might be a while before we see the physical manifestation of the words we are speaking. Looking at Proverbs 18:21, the end of this scripture reads, "And those who love it will eat its fruit".

We all know, in nature, that it takes time for fruit to mature before it's ready to be eaten. We have to realise that this is a concept in God's Kingdom: patience, and fruit takes time. Therefore, we cannot afford to be weary in well-doing.

It is also good practice to meditate on scriptures before we declare them, so we are speaking life from our spirits.

31 DECLARATIONS OF TRUTH

I encourage you to meditate on these scriptures and then declare them over your life.

Enjoy and be blessed.

Bisi

I Have Eternal Life

"And this is the record, that God hath given to us eternal life, and this life is in his Son.

He that hath the Son hath life; and he that hath not the Son of God hath not life. These things have I written unto you that believe on the name of the Son of God; that ye may know that ye have eternal life, and that ye may believe on the name of the Son of God" (1 John 5:11-13; KJV).

I have eternal life because I believe on the name of the Son of God and Christ lives in me. Because

Christ lives in me and this life is in Christ, His life is in me.

That life is manifested in my mortal body (2 Corinthians 4:10), keeping me free from sickness and disease, in Jesus' Name. I also grow gracefully, as I have eternal life abiding in me.

I Am Endued With Power From on High

"Behold, I send the Promise of My Father upon you; but tarry in the city of Jerusalem until you are endued with power from on high" (Luke 24:49).

I have the Holy Spirit with me, and He is the spirit of power (2 Timothy 1:7). As I have the Holy Spirit, I am endued with power from on high.

I am not walking in this life in my own strength; the Holy Spirit strengthens me, and I walk in His power, in Jesus' Name.

"But you shall receive power when the Holy Spirit has come upon you; and you shall be witnesses to Me in Jerusalem, and in all Judea and Samaria, and to the end of the earth" (Acts 1:8).

I am endowed with power from on high to be a good witness of Jesus Christ.

"Now may the God of hope fill you with all joy and peace in believing, that you may abound in hope by the power of the Holy Spirit" (Romans 15:13). I abound in hope by the power of the Holy Spirit.

I Have Received His Fulness

"And of his fulness have all we received, and grace for grace" (John 1:16).

Father, I thank you that I have received the fullness of Christ. I am complete in Him. Your word also says that, "For in him dwelleth all the fulness of the Godhead bodily" (Colossians 2:9). I have God the Father and God the Holy Spirit because the fullness of the Godhead dwells in Christ, and I have received that fullness.

Therefore, I expect to walk in wholeness with a sound mind and a sound body. I can make sound and Spirit-led decisions, in Jesus' Name. The Spirit of God leads me, and I choose to yield to the dwelling of God the Father and God the Holy Spirit, in Jesus' Name.

Called Into the Fellowship of His Son

"God *is* faithful, by whom you were called into the **fellowship** of His Son, Jesus Christ our Lord" (1 Corinthians 1:9).

Father, I thank you that I have been called into the fellowship of Jesus Christ my Lord and Saviour. I can fellowship with the Lord in the spirit as my spirit has been made alive unto God (Romans 6:11).

Father, I also thank you that I have fellowship with you. The scripture says:

"That which we have seen and heard we declare to you, that you also may have **fellowship** with us; and truly our **fellowship** *is* with the Father and with His Son Jesus Christ" (1 John 1:3).

This is a great privilege, and I thank you, Father, that I can fellowship with you and with Jesus Christ, my Lord.

Father, I ask for grace and understanding to experience the depths of what this really means, in Jesus' Name.

The Prince of Peace Lives in Me

"For unto us a Child is born, Unto us a Son is given; And the government will be upon His shoulder. And His name will be called- Wonderful, Counselor, Mighty God, Everlasting Father, **Prince of Peace**" (Isaiah 9:6).

The Prince of Peace lives inside me.

I yield to peace; l live in peace.

I choose peace when the storms of life come.

I stay in peace.

I stay in peace with many.

I have supernatural peace that keeps my heart and mind through Christ Jesus.

I have the greater one in me, and l stay in peace.

The Father of Mercies Is My Father

"Blessed be the God and Father of our Lord Jesus Christ, **the Father of mercies** and God of all comfort" (2 Corinthians 1:3).

The Father of mercies is my Father. Whenever I need mercy, I simply ask for it, and it shall be given unto me.

I walk in mercy; surely goodness and mercy shall follow me all the days of my life.

The tender mercies of God are over all His works.

I have obtained mercy through our Lord Jesus Christ.

I Am a King and Priest Unto God

"And from Jesus Christ, the faithful witness, the firstborn from the dead, and the ruler over the kings of the earth.

To Him who loved us and washed us from our sins in His own blood, and has made us kings and priests to His God and Father, to Him *be* glory and dominion forever and ever. Amen" (Revelation 1:5-6).

Jesus Christ has made me a king and priest unto God.

I reign in life through Jesus Christ, my Lord.

I take my position as a king and priest unto God, in Jesus' Name.

I make decrees, and I intercede for others by standing in the gap for them.

I also offer spiritual sacrifices acceptable to God through Christ Jesus.

The Lord Makes a Way

"Thus says the Lord, who makes a way in the seaAnd a path through the mighty waters,¹ Who brings forth the chariot and horse,The army and the power(They shall lie down together, they shall not rise;They are extinguished, they are quenched like a wick)" (Isaiah 43:16-17).

The Lord makes a way for me.

There is nothing too hard for God.

As I believe Him, I see the Lord do wonders beyond my imagination, in Jesus' Name.

The Path of the Just Shines Brighter and Brighter

"But the path of the just is as the shining light, that shineth more and more unto the perfect day" (Proverbs 4:18 KJV).

"Thy word is a lamp unto my feet, and a light unto my path" (Psalm 119:105).

God's Word is light unto my path.

I study and meditate on God's Word, and the Holy Spirit gives me light and revelation knowledge. That light causes my path to be brighter and brighter unto the coming day.

I walk in the light of life, which gets brighter and brighter every day.

I Reign in Life Through Christ Jesus

"For if by the one man's offense death reigned through the one, much more those who receive abundance of grace and of the gift of righteousness will reign in life through the One, Jesus Christ" (Romans 5:17).

I have received an abundance of grace and the gift of righteousness, and I reign in life through Jesus Christ.

I don't reign in life by striving.

I reign in life by Jesus Christ.

I reign in life through an abundance of grace.

I reign in life through righteousness.

I yield and align myself with God's grace.

I align myself with the gift of righteousness, and l reign in life.

I reign in life because l reign by Jesus Christ, by His grace and the gift of righteousness.

I Have the Mind of Christ

"For who hath known the mind of the Lord, that he may instruct him? but we have the mind of Christ" (1 Corinthians 2:16 KJV).

"For God hath not given us the spirit of fear; but of power, and of love, and of a sound mind" (2 Timothy 1:7 KJV).

I have the mind of Christ.

I have a sound mind all the days of my life.

I process things rightly and correctly, in Jesus' Name.

I Am One Spirit With the Lord

"I in them, and You in Me; that they may be made perfect in one, and that the world may know that You have sent Me, and have loved them as You have loved Me" (John 17:23).

"But he who is joined to the Lord is one spirit *with Him*" (1 Corinthians 6:17).

I am one spirit with the Lord; I have access to His authority and power. Therefore, I can go in the name of the Lord. I can take my authority in His name. I can represent the Lord well because l am one spirit with the Lord.

Surely, Goodness and Mercy Shall Follow Me

"Surely goodness and mercy shall follow meAll the days of my life;And I will dwell in the house of the LordForever" (Psalm 23:6).

Surely, goodness and mercy shall follow me all the days of my life.

I expect the goodness and mercy of God every day to follow me.

The goodness of the Lord overshadows me.

I live from His goodness, and I tell others of His goodness.

It is the goodness of the Lord that leads people to repentance.

Many will see the goodness of the Lord in my life and turn to serve the Lord.

His mercy also follows me every day.

His mercy triumphs over judgment.

His mercy preserves me.

The mercy of the Lord defends me and speaks for me in places that l cannot reach.

His goodness and mercy go before me and prepare the way before me.

In Christ, l have obtained mercy.

His goodness leads me to repentance.

No Condemnation in Christ Jesus

"*There is* therefore now no condemnation to those who are in Christ Jesus, who do not walk according to the flesh, but according to the Spirit" (Romans 8:1).

There is no condemnation for those in Christ Jesus.

I do not walk after the flesh, but I walk after the Spirit.

I am sensitive to the promptings of the Holy Spirit.

When l miss it, l ask the Lord to forgive me, and He does.

I also forgive myself and move on.

I refuse to walk in condemnation.

Jesus has paid the price for me, and I walk in the reality of His finished work.

I walk in freedom towards God and man.

Christ Is Glorified in Me

"And all Mine are Yours, and Yours are Mine, and I am glorified in them" (John 17:10).

That the name of our Lord Jesus Christ may be glorified in you, and you in Him, according to the grace of our God and the Lord Jesus Christ (2 Thessalonians 1:12).

Jesus Christ is glorified in me.

The name of the Lord Jesus Christ is glorified in me.

Everything that the name above all names represents is reflected in me.

It is reflected in my life and my sphere of influence.

I represent the Lord Jesus Christ well, and He is glorified in me.

I am hidden in Christ, and I am glorified in Him.

This is all according to His ability and His grace.

Joint Heirs With Christ

"The Spirit Himself bears witness with our spirit that we are children of God, ¹⁷ and if children, then heirs—heirs of God and joint heirs with Christ, if indeed we suffer with *Him,* that we may also be glorified together" (Romans 8:16-17).

I am an heir of God and a joint heir with Christ.

I have an inheritance in Christ (Ephesians 1:11).

I have inherited what Jesus Christ inherited.

Jesus was given a name above all names by inheritance (Hebrews 1:4), and that name belongs to me (Acts 3:6; Mark 16:17).

The glory that God gave to Jesus, Jesus Christ my Lord and Saviour, has been given to me:

"And the glory which You gave Me I have given them, that they may be one just as We are one" (John 17:22).

Father, thank you that I am your heir and joint heir with Christ.

Partaker of the Heavenly Calling

"Therefore, holy brethren, **partakers of the heavenly calling**, consider the Apostle and High Priest of our confession, Christ Jesus" (Hebrews 3:1).

I press toward the mark for the prize of the high calling of God in Christ Jesus (Philippians 3:14).

I am a partaker of the heavenly calling.

I walk in the consciousness that l have been called to be a saint (Romans 1:7).

I am called to be God's people.

"Who hath saved me and called me with an holy **calling**, not according to my our works, but according to his own purpose and grace, which was given me in Christ Jesus before the world began" (2 Timothy 1:9).

I have been called in Christ Jesus before the world began.

By the grace of God, I will discover my purpose, in Jesus' Name and walk in its manifestation, bringing glory to God and mankind, in Jesus' Name.

Seated in Heavenly Places With Christ

But God, who is rich in mercy, because of His great love with which He loved us, even when we were dead in trespasses, made us alive together with Christ (by grace you have been saved), **and raised *us* up together, and made *us* sit together in the heavenly *places* in Christ Jesus** (Ephesians 2:4-6).

I have been raised together and sit together in the heavenly places in Christ Jesus.

As I am in Christ, when Christ was raised, I was raised with Him.

I am now seated in heavenly places in Christ Jesus.

When I pray, I pray from my seated position in Christ Jesus.

This is a place of authority in Christ.

When I pray, I pray from my position in Christ.

Jesus achieved this for me, and I am simply a beneficiary because I am now in Christ.

I pray from this reality, and things happen, in Jesus' Name.

The Lord Is My Helper

"*Let your* conduct *be* without covetousness; *be* content with such things as you have. For He Himself has said, "I will never leave you nor forsake you." So we may boldly say:

"The Lord *is* my helper; I will not fear. What can man do to me?" (Hebrews 13:5-6).

The Lord is my helper.

The Lord helps me.

I do not live in this life in my own strength.

One reason that God sent Jesus Christ is so that l can live through Him (1 John 4:9).

Indeed, the Lord is my helper.

According to Psalm 121, my help comes from the Lord who made heaven and earth.

The Blessing of Abraham

"In your seed all the nations of the earth shall be blessed, because you have obeyed My voice" (Genesis 22:18).

"I will bless those who bless you, And I will curse him who curses you; And in you all the families of the earth shall be blessed" (Genesis 12:3).

My family is blessed because of Abraham.

I call my seed blessed.

They will find their God-ordained destiny in Christ, walk in it, and bless many, in Jesus' Name.

I call my family blessed, in Jesus' Name.

My seed will walk in their God-ordained purpose and receive eternal rewards, in Jesus' Name.

I Will Not Bring Forth for Sorrow

"They shall not labor in vain, Nor bring forth children for trouble; For they *shall be* the descendants of the blessed of the Lord, And their offspring with them" (Isaiah 65:23).

I will not labour in vain nor bring forth for trouble.

All my children shall be taught of the Lord, and great shall be the peace of my children.

BISI OLADIPUPO

My children are taught of the Lord, and they walk in His ways.

My children shall be carriers of peace.

Peace with God and peace with men.

My offspring shall be a channel of peace.

As He Is, so Are We in This World

"Love has been perfected among us in this: that we may have boldness in the day of judgment; because as He is, so are we in this world." (1 John 4:17).

As Christ is, so am l in this world.

I work in the authority given to me in Christ.

I represent Christ on this earth.

My life will bring glory to the Lord Jesus Christ in this life.

I yield to the leading of the Holy Spirit as Jesus Christ did during His earthly ministry.

I yield to the fruit of the Spirit daily in my life.

I have fellowship with God the Father.

I obey the voice of the Holy Spirit.

I release the kingdom of God to my sphere of influence.

I seek the kingdom of God and His righteousness.

Because as He is, so am I in this world.

I Am a Chosen Generation, a Royal Priesthood, a Holy Nation, a Peculiar People

"But ye are a chosen generation, a royal priesthood, an holy nation, a peculiar people; that ye should shew forth the praises of him who hath called you out of darkness into his marvellous light" (1 Peter 2:9; KJV).

But you are a chosen race, a royal priesthood, a consecrated nation, a [special] people for *God's* own possession, so that you may proclaim the excellencies [the wonderful deeds and virtues and perfections] of Him who called you out of darkness into His marvelous light (1 Peter 2:9; AMP).

I am a chosen generation.

Chosen in Christ.

A royal priesthood by the sacrifice of Jesus.

A holy nation by the sacrifice of Jesus.

A peculiar people through the sacrifice of Jesus.

I have been called to proclaim the praises of the Lord.

I have been called out of darkness.

I am now a partaker of His marvellous light.

Marvellous light in Christ.

The Spirit of Truth Dwells in Me

"And I will pray the Father, and He will give you another Helper, that He may abide with you forever— the Spirit of truth, whom the world cannot receive, because it neither sees Him nor knows Him; but you know Him, for He dwells with you and will be in you" (John 14:16-17).

The Holy Spirit is the Spirit of truth.

He guides me into all truth.

He shows me things to come.

He is also the spirit of power, and of love, and of a sound mind (2 Timothy 1:7).

The love of God has been shed abroad in my heart by the Holy Spirit (Romans 5:5).

The Holy Spirit bears witness with my spirit that I am a child of God (Romans 8:16).

I Am the Righteousness of God in Christ Jesus

"For He made Him who knew no sin *to be* sin for us, that we might become the righteousness of God in Him" (2 Corinthians 5:21).

I have been made right with God through the sacrifice of Jesus Christ.

I have a right standing with God.

I am the righteousness of God in Christ.

This righteousness is by faith in Christ Jesus.

I now live consciously that in the sight of God I am righteous because of Jesus Christ, as I am now in Christ.

The Grace of God Is at Work in Me

"To this *end* I also labor, striving according to His working which works in me mightily" (Colossians 1:29).

"But by the grace of God I am what I am, and His grace toward me was not in vain; but I labored more abundantly than they all, yet not I, but the grace of God *which was* with me" (1 Corinthians 15:10).

"Whereof I was made a minister, according to the gift of the grace of God given unto me by the effectual working of his power" (Ephesians 3:7; KJV).

Insert your name and gifting:

Whereof _____ was made a _____ , according to the gift of the grace of God given unto me by the effectual working of His power.

Father, I thank you for your gift that was given unto me by your grace. That grace is working mightily in my life by your power.

Your grace is with me, and as I yield to that grace, there is no need to strive. Your grace is at work mightily in me by your power, in Jesus' Name.

The Generation of the Upright Is Blessed

"Praise the Lord!

Blessed *is* the man *who* fears the Lord, *Who* delights greatly in His commandments.

His descendants will be mighty on earth; The generation of the upright will be blessed. Wealth and riches *will be* in his house, And his righteousness endures forever" (Psalm 112:1-3).

I walk in the fear of the Lord. I delight greatly in His commandments; the Word of God is my delight, and my descendants shall be mighty upon the earth.

I call my generation blessed of the Lord.

I call my descendants blessed of the Lord.

Jesus Loves Me as the Father Loves Jesus

"As the Father loved Me, I also have loved you; abide in My love" (John 15:9).

"I in them, and You in Me; that they may be made perfect in one, and that the world may know that You have sent Me, and have loved them as You have loved Me" (John 17:23).

Jesus loves me with the same love as the Father loves Jesus.

God the Father loves me as He loves Jesus Christ.

I walk in the security of the love of God for me.

God's love towards me is steadfast and endures forever.

God wants the best for me.

God Always Causes Me to Triumph in Christ

"Now thanks be unto God, which always causeth us to triumph in Christ, and maketh manifest the savour of his knowledge by us in every place" (2 Corinthians 2:14; KJV).

"Now thanks *be* to God who always leads us in triumph in Christ, and through us diffuses the fragrance of His knowledge in every place" (2 Corinthians 2:14).

God always causes me to triumph in Christ Jesus.
I always expect to win in Christ.

I Am Crucified With Christ

"I am crucified with Christ: nevertheless I live; yet not I, but Christ liveth in me: and the life which I now live in the flesh I live by the faith of the Son of God, who loved me, and gave himself for me" (Galatians 2:20 KJV).

"I am crucified with Christ, the life that l now live in the flesh l live by faith of the Son of God. Christ now lives in me. I live this life through Christ."

This is one reason that God sent Jesus Christ, that I might live through Him.

"In this the love of God was manifested toward us, that God has sent His only begotten Son into the world, that we might live through Him" (1 John 4:9).

I don't need to strive in this life; I have help as I live through Christ. He helps me, strengthens me, and gives me victory. I was crucified with Him. I have victory over the works of the flesh through the sacrifice of Christ.

According to the book of Romans, Chapter six, sin shall not have dominion over me, for I am not under the law but under grace.

God Is Not Withholding His Will From Me

"Having made known to us the mystery of His will, according to His good pleasure which He purposed in Himself" (Ephesians 1:9).

God is not withholding His will from me. It is His good pleasure to make known the mystery of His will.

As I seek the Lord and align myself, He reveals His will for His kingdom and for my life to me.

God loves me so much, and He is not withholding any good thing from me.

The scriptures tell me in the book of Ephesians, chapter five, verse seventeen, "Therefore do not be unwise, but understand what the will of the Lord *is*".

The Lord wants me to know His will so I can walk in wisdom.

By His grace, I align myself, and I walk in wisdom, knowing the will of God, in Jesus' Name.

Acknowledgements

Firstly, I want to acknowledge my Lord and Saviour Jesus Christ, the giver of gifts.

Thank you Lord your grace of writing.

About the author

For many years, Bisi Oladipupo has been a Christian and lives in the UK with her family. She's a graduate of multiple Bible colleges, including a UK leadership program. Additionally, she graduated from a U.S. ministry school with a Bachelor's degree in Bible and Theology. Bisi teaches God's Word and leads Bible studies and Christian fellowship groups. Visit her website and author page located at www.bisiwrites.com and www.bisiwrites.org.

Bisi can be reached at bisiwriter@gmail.com for enquiries.

Salvation Prayer

Father God, I come to you in Jesus' name. I admit that I am a sinner, and I now receive the sacrifice that Jesus Christ paid for me.

I confess with my mouth the Lord Jesus, and I believe in my heart that God raised Him from the dead.

I now declare that Jesus Christ is my Lord and Saviour.

Thank you, Father, for saving me in Jesus' name.

I am now your child. Amen.

If you've said this prayer for the first time, please send an email to Bisiwriter@gmail.com.

Start reading your Bible and ask the Lord to guide you to a good church. Additionally, ask the Lord for good Christian friends who will support and help you along this new journey.

Also by Bisi

1. The Twelve Apostles of Jesus Christ: Lessons We Can Learn

2. The Lord's Cup in Communion: The Significance of taking the Lord's Supper

3. Different Ways to Receive Healing from Scripture and Walk in Health

4. Believing on The Name of Jesus Christ: What Every Believer Needs to Know

5. The Mind and Your Christian Walk: The Impact of the mind on our Christian walk

6. Relationship Skills in the Bible: Scriptural Principles of relating to others

7. The Nature of God's Kingdom: The Characteristics of the Kingdom of God

8. The Person of the Holy Spirit

9. 41 Insights from the Book of Revelation

10. The Importance of Spiritual Discernment

11. God Speaks Through Nature

12. It's All About the Heart

13. A Better Covenant: A Look at the Covenants of God and Our Better Covenant

14. 40 Day New Covenant Devotional

15. What Happens When We Pray?

16. Daily Bread for Healing: A 40-day Healing Devotional

17. 40 Facts of Who Jesus Is: A Devotional

18. 50 Prayers for Your Children and Generations to Come

19. The Grace of God: Why We Need It

20. The Importance of Spiritual Understanding

21. In Christ: Who We Are and What We Have in Him : 40 Daily Bites

22. Inspired Poems Volume 1

23. Inspired Poems Volume 2

Afterword

If you enjoyed this book, please take a few moments to write a review of it online at the store where it was purchased. Thank you.

www.ingramcontent.com/pod-product-compliance
Lightning Source LLC
Chambersburg PA
CBHW022213090526
44584CB00013BA/862